C000153346

TAXES FOR SMALL BUSINESSES

QuickStart Guide

Understanding Taxes For Your Sole Proprietorship, Startup, & LLC

Copyright 2016 by ClydeBank Media - All Rights Reserved.

This document is geared towards providing exact and reliable information in regards to the topic and issue covered. The publication is sold with the idea that the publisher is not required to render accounting, officially permitted, or otherwise, qualified services. If advice is necessary, legal or professional, a practiced individual in the profession should be ordered.

From a Declaration of Principles which was accepted and approved equally by a Committee of the American Bar Association and a Committee of Publishers and Associations. In no way is it legal to reproduce, duplicate, or transmit any part of this document in either electronic means or in printed format. Recording of this publication is strictly prohibited and any storage of this document is not allowed unless with written permission from the publisher.

The information provided herein is stated to be truthful and consistent, in that any liability, in terms of inattention or otherwise, by any usage or abuse of any policies, processes, or directions contained within is the solitary and utter responsibility of the recipient reader. Under no circumstances will any legal responsibility or blame be held against the publisher for any reparation, damages, or monetary loss due to the information herein, either directly or indirectly. Respective authors own all copyrights not held by the publisher. The information herein is offered for informational purposes solely, and is universal as so. The presentation of the information is without contract or any type of guarantee assurance.

Trademarks: All trademarks are the property of their respective owners. The trademarks that are used are without any consent, and the publication of the trademark is without permission or backing by the trademark owner. All trademarks and brands within this book are for clarifying purposes only and are owned by the owners themselves, not affiliated with this document.

Disclaimer: The author of this book is not a lawyer. Additionally, the publisher of this book does not intend this text to serve as legal advice. The complex legal subjects presented here should be considered 'simplifications' in a legal advice sense and are not case-specific. If you are seeking legal advice, please contact an attorney who is well-versed in business law as neither the author nor the publisher is a lawyer.

ClydeBank Media LLC is not associated with any organization, product or service discussed in this book. The publisher has made every effort to ensure that the information presented in this book was accurate at time of publication. All precautions have been taken in the preparation of this book. The publisher, author, editor and designer assume no responsibility for any loss, damage, or disruption caused by errors or omissions from this book, whether such errors or omissions result from negligence, accident, or any other cause.

Edition # 1 – Updated : April 14, 2016

Cover Illustration and Design: Katie Poorman, Copyright © 2016 by ClydeBank Media LLC
Interior Design: Katie Poorman, Copyright © 2016 by ClydeBank Media LLC

Copyright © 2016
ClydeBank Media LLC
www.clydebankmedia.com
All Rights Reserved

ISBN-13 : 978-1-945051-21-0

contents

BEFORE YOU START READING, DOWNLOAD YOUR FREE DIGITAL ASSETS!

Visit the URL below to access your free Digital Asset files that are included with the purchase of this book.

☑ Summaries   ☑ White Papers
☑ Cheat Sheets   ☑ Charts & Graphs
☑ Articles   ☑ Reference Materials

DOWNLOAD YOURS HERE:

www.clydebankmedia.com/taxes-assets

introduction

Taxes are a significant expenditure for any business, large or small. They must be readily considered and incorporated into your business plan from the very beginning. Understanding them, however, can be a chore.

Benjamin Franklin said, "In this world, nothing can be certain except death and taxes", and taxes can be a whole lot more complicated than death.

The typical small business owner works three to four months just to earn enough profit to pay taxes. As a matter of fact, the largest single expense for most small business owners is their annual tax bill. But that's all part of operating your own business, and the process of planning for, collecting, and paying taxes needn't be complicated. The basic information offered in this book will provide you with the material you need to maximize your understanding of a variety of tax laws and to keep you in compliance and out of trouble.

Though you may be inclined to want to turn all of your tax questions, issues, and problems over to an accountant, it's still important for you - the small business owner – to understand the ins and outs of the U.S. tax system. However, it's also essential to recognize that this is an ever-changing system, full of modifications that seem to come out almost annually. That means staying in the loop might require some regular education and research as well as consultations with any tax professional you might hire.

| 1 |

The Basics

Simply put, you're required by law each year to complete the tax forms that pertain to your business. You MUST complete these forms or you face penalties from the various entities that demand the reporting. There are deadlines for filing each as well, so it's important to get a handle on what's due and when it should be submitted.

It all starts with good accounting.

Cash vs. Accrual-Based Accounting

Formally speaking, it is proper for businesses to choose and rely on **accrual-based accounting** rather than **cash-based accounting** for generating financial reports to submit to banks, partners, and other parties, but, when it comes to reporting tax liability, cash-based accounting is the preferred method. (If you're not clear on the difference see the Glossary of Terms at the end of this text.) The important thing to know is that many well-run businesses need to maintain two distinct accounting record systems: an accrual system for their business and financial management and a cash system to determine their appropriate tax liabilities.

Just as is the case when filing personal taxes, you'll be filing your business tax returns at various levels.

The Federal Level

Federal taxation is primarily focused on taxing the profits (or income) of your small business. Though the state you live in may also collect income tax (not all states do), the largest income tax you pay is to the federal government.

If you have employees, you must submit your employees' tax withholdings to the federal government, along with your share of payroll taxes, including 50% of the Medicare and Social Security taxes, as well as FUTA-based taxes, which are reviewed in detail in Chapter 3.

If you're filing on your own without help from a tax preparer, you may find yourself a bit confused about which forms to use.

Here is a quick overview:

- *Sole Proprietorships* file a Form 1040 and a Schedule C or C-EZ, depending on your expenses. If you are a farm business, you also need to file a Schedule F.

- *Partnerships* file a Form 1065 to report their incomes, gains, losses, and deductions. A partnership does not pay tax on its income but, rather, passes through profits and losses to its partners.

- *C Corporations* are taxed as separate entities and must file annually via a Form 1120.

- *S Corporations* are pass-through entities (see more about this in the next chapter). Shareholders of S Corporations report the flow-through of income and losses on their personal tax returns and are assessed at their individual tax rates. Nonetheless, an informational Form 1120S must be filed.

- *Limited Liability Companies* that are single-member LLCs file Form 1040 along with a Schedule C, E, or F, whereas multiple-member LLCs need to file a Form 1065.

Forms 1120, 1120S, and 1120A are due to the IRS by March 15th of each year for the previous year. Forms 1040 (and its variants), Schedule C, and Form 1065 are due to the IRS by April 15th.

If you're tackling this without help, companies such as Turbo Tax offer good guidance, or you may call the IRS or log onto their website for more specific information.

The State Level

Each state in the U.S. has its own set of tax laws. Your tax requirements for your state largely depend on your business structure (LLC, sole proprietorship, S corporation, etc.).

Businesses with employees are required to pay employment taxes. All states, for example, demand taxes associated with unemployment insurance and workers' compensation insurance.

In addition to taking their share of income taxes, states tend to rely heavily on collecting *sales taxes*. If you sell goods or services (as most do), then you are responsible for collecting sales tax and submitting the revenue to your state's Board of Equalization according to the timetable mandated by your state authority.

States also collect what's known as *use tax*, which is a type of excise tax on a good or service purchased outside the state for which no sales tax was collected. The internet shopping company, Amazon, recently brought up the issue of use tax for discussion since many products purchased on Amazon are sold without the addition of sales tax. As a rule, if the item purchased for use by your small business is not a food item and would have been taxed had it been sold in your state, then you owe your Board of Equalization a use tax for that item.

If the business is purchasing items for retail sale, then no sales tax needs to be paid. The sales tax is collected when the item is sold to the end consumer.

Note : If a small business owner gives to himself or someone else merchandise that was purchased for retail sale, then the small business owner is required to pay a use tax for that item, as it was purchased without paying sales tax and then used by the business owner as a gift (to himself or someone else).

Websites for the government of each state offer tax information for those who are trying to decipher the tax laws of their particular locales.

The County Level

Businesses that own real property in a particular county (land or buildings) generally pay county taxes. The county also collects taxes on property the business owns, such as vehicles or other physical goods.

The City Level

Last but not least, if the business is up and running in a city, then that city may request that the business cough up some cash for a license to operate in that city. This expense isn't, relatively speaking, a hugely expensive one, but since it's being paid to a government entity in exchange for governmental recognition and protection (city police), it constitutes a tax.

Reasons to Prepare Your Own Tax Returns

Small businesses, especially those just starting out, don't always have a lot of expendable income. That means most owners are generally searching for ways to save dollars, and preparing your own taxes is one of those ways to keep annual expenses in check.

With good record keeping, tackling your own tax returns isn't confusing or frustrating. Software programs such as QuickBooks© actually make it very easy to keep track of income, expenses, deductions, and everything else you'll need in order to fill in your federal forms as well as those at the state, county, or city level. Furthermore, most business returns don't vary a lot from year to year, unless you make some sort of major change. Often, you can follow the return from the year before, inserting new numbers and allowing for any changes in the tax code.

Indeed, there are several advantages to preparing your own taxes. First of all, it allows you to get a good overall picture of your business. If you're busy with the day-in and day-out burdens of running the business, it may be rare that you sit down and take a look at the health of your business, determining what's working and what's not. Preparing your own taxes forces you to take that look…and you may be surprised at what you find.

Similarly, a close look at tax returns for each year allows you to make better financial decisions for the future, because you'll gain so much knowledge about the tax system and how it affects your business.

Also, doing your own taxes forces you to stay up-to-date on the latest changes to the tax system. It might require a little more reading time, but you'll find it'll be worth it in the long run if it helps you to avoid costly mistakes.

The best part is, you'll save lots of money! CBS Money Watch estimates that the average small business in Middle America pays about $450 to have a Form 1040 and Schedule C prepared.cite Prices are generally higher in other parts of the country, such as New York, New England, and California. That price doesn't count preparation of taxes at other levels (state, county) and any other services you might require.

Choosing the Right Tax Preparer

If after considering the pros and cons of preparing your own tax returns you decide that it's better left to the experts, then you'll need to find the right expert for you.

Remember, not everyone who hangs a tax preparer shingle outside her business is a tax expert and, certainly, not all of them know the particulars of filing for various types of businesses. So, you don't necessarily want to choose your neighbor who "does taxes" or Uncle John who was a bookkeeper. It takes time to find the right person.

There are four types of tax practitioners available to help your tax needs.

An Unenrolled Preparer

These individuals have the minimum amount of training necessary to tackle your returns. These are the people you'll usually find working at H&R Block or other well-known national tax preparation firms. These preparers don't need to be licensed, though they've likely had to complete some training in order to be hired. There's a very good chance, however, that many of them don't have a good working knowledge of business taxes, though their services may be ideal for someone who only requires a simple form for their personal taxes. Furthermore, hiring someone from a firm in a mall, for example, means you'll only have access to him during tax season and not year-round.

Enrolled Agents

An enrolled agent must undergo longer and more rigorous training than her unenrolled counterparts and must also engage in yearly continuing education in order to update her license. They are ideal for tax preparation and basic advice and can represent you at an audit. Their cost is generally less than if you hired a CPA.

Certified Public Accountants (CPAs)

CPAs must undergo extensive training and pass difficult tests in order to obtain their certifications. Furthermore, they must complete an additional 40 hours of training each year to maintain that certification. Their services can be quite expensive. Note that in many cases, unless you expect your returns to be very complicated or if your business underwent some significant changes during the past year, you probably don't need a CPA to do your taxes. Hiring one is likely to be a huge waste of hard-earned dollars.

Tax Attorneys

Similar to hiring CPAs, hiring a tax attorney for a small business is probably overkill. You'll find yourself paying huge hourly rates for tasks that can as easily be done by an enrolled agent or other preparer.

Choosing a tax preparer needn't be a daunting task. It's always a good idea to seek referrals from other similar small businesses in your area, especially those who've been in business for a long time. And remember, if you use someone one time and aren't pleased, you don't have to use him again. There are plenty of preparers out there. You just need to find the one that best suits your needs and your budget. So take time to ask questions as you interview potential candidates, and don't be afraid to say "no" if the fit just doesn't seem right.

| 2 |

Choosing the Correct Entity

One of the most common mistakes small businesses make is failing to choose an appropriate business entity and keeping the expenses and accounts of that entity separate from the business owner's personal expenses and accounts. When you begin your business, consider the various entity options and think about the possible advantages and disadvantages of each of the various business types.

Basic Entities

Sole Proprietorships

These are single-owner entities whose owners hold full personal responsibility for the liabilities of the business. The income generated from a *sole proprietorship* is recorded on the federal Schedule C form and then relayed to the owner's 1040 form. The sole proprietorship is thus considered a "pass-through entity". The main advantage of the sole proprietorship is that it's really easy to set up. All you technically have to do is open up for business and you're automatically considered a sole proprietorship. The downside, of course, is being personally liable for the business. If someone were to fall, slip and break her back on the floor of your donut shop and you are found liable, then you could potentially lose everything you own - your house, your car, your savings, not to mention your business.

Partnership (general & limited)

Partnerships are formed by two or more individuals who decide to go into business together. In general partnerships, the parties going into business are personally liable for the debts and legal judgments levied against the business, while in limited partnerships and "limited liability" partnerships, certain owners may not be held personally liable for the actions of the business. Partnerships represent another example of pass-through taxation, because the partnership's profit is passed onto its owners, who report the income on their personal tax records.

C Corporations

C corporations insulate their owners or shareholders from personal liability. For tax purposes, C corporations can be a little cumbersome. The corporation is taxed as an entity unto itself (this is an example of a non-pass-through entity) and the profits distributed to the C corporation's shareholders are also taxed as personal income. Therefore, the same money is actually being taxed twice. Many smaller businesses, especially in the United States where the corporate tax is relatively high, opt for the S corporation to avoid this double taxation.

S Corporation

Like C corporations, *S corporations* insulate their owners and shareholders from personal liability. But unlike C corporations, S corporations are *pass-through entities*. Profits and losses are passed through to the shareholder's personal tax returns and there is, thus, no double taxation.

LLCs

LLCs or *Limited Liability Companies* are pass-through entities that can be owned by one or multiple parties. LLCs insulate their owners from liability.

> *Note : With C corporations, S corporations, LLCs, and limited partnerships, certain actions undertaken by their members and owners in the name of the company may, at times, make them personally liable. This phenomenon is known as "piercing the corporate veil". If, for example, a company's owners were deliberately reckless with their spending, amassing unneeded debt, then a court could elect to pierce the corporate veil and hold the owners personally responsible to the creditors if the company can't pay.*

When choosing the entity best suited for your business you should consider the distinctive advantages of each entity. Many business owners who do not have significant personal assets elect to form sole proprietorships. There are a host of small conveniences associated with the sole proprietorship, as well as some built-in goodies that can create a remarkably better experience for the business owner. With a sole proprietorship, you can write off your health care premiums and you can take advantage of certain benefits that come from hiring family members (described in more detail in Chapter 6). You also have the convenience of not having to file a separate return for your business. Just attach your Schedule C to your personal tax return and off you go!

Partnerships give business owners an added degree of tax flexibility, which can in some cases result in savings. Partners in a business may move assets around within the partnership. Property may be "assigned" from one partner to the next, along with income or debt. The business can structure and assign its way to a lower tax liability with ease. For example, if one person in the partnership is right on the cusp of moving into a more expensive income tax bracket, then having the flexibility to assign that partner less income from the partnership instantly results in tax savings. With partnerships it is also possible to completely discharge assets out of the business and give them to a partner without owing property disbursement taxes.

Small businesses, by and large, prefer S corporations to C corporations, because they're usually not dealing with public companies and can't really justify getting taxed once at the business entity level and then again at the personal level after the business distributes its profits.

Note : Usually, C corporations become justified when the owners of the business are wealthy and therefore taxed in a very high tax bracket. The C corporation is taxed at the entity level before its dividends are distributed, and the corporate tax rate is often quite a bit lower than the income tax rate for wealthier individuals. Therefore, it benefits certain individuals to have at least some of their earnings taxed at the corporate rate, reducing the total amount that would have been taxed at the individual income rate. With a pass-through entity, all of the business's earnings are taxed at the individual income rate.

In addition to getting some liability protection, one nice thing about having an S corporation as opposed to a partnership or sole proprietorship is that you don't have to pay the dreadfully expensive self-employment tax.

The LLC, a relatively new form of business entity, is heavily influenced by the particulars of state law. It is thus difficult to make a determination on the benefits of choosing the LLC entity unless you brush up on the laws in your state. In general, LLCs offer the same flexibility in profit and asset distribution as partnerships, but with added liability protection. An LLC may also be formed by a single individual business owner. This is known as a single-member LLC.

One universal tenet, regardless of which entity you choose for your business, is to be sure to clearly separate the business entity from the owners. Keep a separate business checking account and business credit cards. Keep all property used by the business in the name of the business. The IRS does not reward business owners who keep confusing records in which the lines between the personal and the business are not clearly maintained.

| 3 |

The IRS & Your Small Business

The IRS has been portrayed by the media as a villainous, soulless organization eager to steamroll its way through your life and livelihood. The IRS is often unjustly blamed for the complexity of the tax code, even though they don't write it— politicians do. In truth, the IRS can be extremely flexible, even friendly and empathic. Remember, they essentially have to deal with the same complex tax paperwork and calculations as your business. Most IRS officials would rejoice at the idea of a simpler tax code.

Rest assured that the chances of your small business being audited are slim. According to IRS statistics, the government agency audits only approximately 3-5% of all sole proprietorships and about 2% of all small corporations.

You can decrease your chances of raising any red flags by following a few essential principals that will keep you out of the limelight.

Dealing with the IRS

Always Follow Their Timelines/Deadlines
Even if you're not sure whether or not you've used a form correctly, and if you can't pay the amount that's due, you should make contact with the IRS. In other words, file by your file date. As long as the IRS hears from you, they're less incentivized to use their limited manpower to audit you. In reality, you're already self-auditing by giving an account of your predicament in accordance with the appropriate time frame. That means you're saving them the work and saving yourself from a potential official audit.

21

Be Careful with Your Deductions & Expenses

Make sure that what you claim as a business expense is really a *business expense*. Just because you flew to Jamaica with your girlfriend for a vacation and took a couple business calls while lying out on the beach with your Pina Colada, this *does not* mean that you were on a business trip. If you have excessive expenses that don't seem to jive well with the amount of revenue you're claiming, then your tax return is more likely to get flagged for further unwanted attention. An IRS screener looks over your expenses, the amounts and the types, and evaluates whether the numbers seem logical. For instance, if you're running an auto repair garage and are trying to claim a home office exemption with lots of deductions for meals and entertainment, then you might run into a bit of trouble. Use your head and don't try to "get away" with claiming extraneous expenses.

Don't Underreport

The IRS uses a program called ***Automated Under-reporter Program***, which matches up data submitted on tax returns to data submitted from third parties. For example, a person's individual income tax return may be compared against records submitted from the person's employer. If there is a discrepancy, the tax return will be flagged and examined.

Keep the IRS Informed of Your Whereabouts

According to the law, the IRS is required to send important and often time-sensitive notices to the address they have on file for you. If they do not have a current address and their notices go unanswered or time periods lapse, then they're more likely to take heavy-handed approaches when it comes time to pay the piper. You've got to keep the IRS alert to the present whereabouts of your business (your business's mailing address). Use the IRS form 8822, which you can download from IRS.gov, when you change your address.

Remaining in Good Standing with the IRS

An important rule to follow when dealing with the IRS is to avoid a situation in which the IRS is using manpower to track you down or to collect information about you. You should ALWAYS be proactive in getting information to the IRS, thus remaining in their good graces.

You can do this by filing on time, notifying the IRS when you change your address, and making sure that, when you file, you do so as accurately as possible. Even if you can't pay what you owe, be proactive in getting it on record that you owe a certain amount, that you're aware of your obligations, and that you intend to pay it back. If you take these steps, the IRS will essentially allow you to self-manage your tax issues.

Business owners may be tempted, when they know they can't pay, to not file at all and just hope that the IRS doesn't notice. This is not a wise plan of action. Such behavior can skyrocket and turn into a burgeoning problem. Often, those who don't file/pay and hear nothing from the IRS assume they've gotten away with something. Some assume their business is too small for the IRS to notice, so they continue failing to file or pay. It's a cycle that could continue for some time until the IRS figures out something is amiss.

The unfortunate reality is that pretending that taxes don't exist eventually catches up with you and can be devastating for your business. The IRS eventually files your taxes for you. When the IRS does this, it's known as filing a *substitute for return* or SFR. The IRS uses whatever available information they have to create your return and assess your tax burden. It may or may not be accurate.

Note : Some individuals and businesses that would have otherwise been entitled to refunds still don't file. A taxpayer's eligibility for a refund expires after 3 years.

Understanding Your Rights

If you find yourself behind on taxes or in the cross-hairs of an IRS audit, you have certain rights. First and foremost, you have an opportunity to present your side of the situation, but the burden of proof is on you. Before you choose to attend an audit on your own, truly assess whether or not you can handle it. You have the right to hire an accountant or an attorney to represent your interests during the audit process. The IRS may discourage you from involving a third party, as this often makes their job slower and more difficult, but it could very well be advantageous to you - the tax payer.

Furthermore, if you attend an audit by yourself or with your business partner(s) and you become overwhelmed by the process and are in over your head, you have the right to demand that the audit be suspended until you have the opportunity to speak with a tax professional. This will indeed delay the whole process but might be to your advantage in the long run.

What the IRS Auditor Wants

Remember, not everyone who is chosen for audit is pegged as a tax cheater. Sometimes information from you and third parties (i.e. your employees) doesn't match up, perhaps due to error on the part of the other party or even due to an input mistake by the IRS. So it's important not to approach the audit as if you have something to hide or for which you must be forgiven.

When an IRS official is assigned to your business to conduct an audit, her main objective is to get the case closed as fast as possible and to convince you, the taxpayer, to agree to her findings. Your auditor, in most cases, accepts a few modifications to her findings if making the modifications means that you readily agree to them. It's better for the auditor to bring back a less aggressive report that was agreed upon promptly than to bring back a very aggressive report that's unsigned by the taxpayer.

While you shouldn't try to be sneaky and swindle your way out of a liability that you rightfully owe, you must not, under any circumstances, be afraid to stand up for yourself if you think the audit findings are not just. Keep a cooperative, communicative dialog running with your IRS auditing official. She is open to negotiation. If you're unable to agree, then request that your case be forwarded to the IRS's Appeals Division.

The IRS Statute of Limitations

Generally, the IRS goes through the last three years of records. So, why are we told to always keep records from at least five years back? If the IRS identifies a potentially significant error, then they may inspect records that go back further, but usually no more than six years at most.

Note : The only exception comes in the case of fraud, in which case the IRS may go back in time indefinitely. There is essentially no statute of limitations if the IRS has reasonable cause to believe your business is guilty of tax fraud.

In some cases, an audit is in progress just as the statute of limitations is expiring - the point at which the IRS is no longer legally permitted to audit the return. If this is the case, then the IRS may ask you to agree to an extension of the statute of limitations. While you don't have to agree to the extension, it may be in your interest to do so. If you refuse, then the auditing team will likely try to wrap up the examination before the statute of limitations expires, and this may not allow you sufficient time to gather and present evidence in your favor.

The next chapter discusses one of the most important assets you have when facing an audit: *good record keeping*.

| 4 |

How to Keep Good Records

A business that keeps excellent records gets through any audit quickly and painlessly. Even if your business is benefitting from the services of a tax professional—an accountant or an attorney—you still need to keep good records on a daily basis.

What to Keep & For How Long

A lot of experts differ on what you should or shouldn't keep as far as receipts, bank statements, and other paperwork pertinent to your business. You definitely need to strike a balance. You don't want to be so paranoid of an audit that you wind up with boxes and boxes of documents, many of which you'll never need. In the long run saving too much creates clutter and makes things more difficult for you during an audit. Certain items may be shredded annually or monthly, such as ATM receipts that are already noted on your bank statement. If the paperwork doesn't contain evidence of a deductible business expense, then you can get rid of it.

When making purchases that are business related, set up a filing system and keep these receipts for four years. Also keep receipts for deductible charitable contributions for four years, as well as any other documentation that can be used to support the information as it appears on your tax return, including the items on the following page:

- Canceled checks
- Mileage logs
- Credit card statements
- Invoices

- Cash register tapes
- Bank deposit slips
- 1099s and W2s

Though the IRS recommends keeping tax returns for six years, some tax professionals advise keeping returns forever. They don't really take up much space, and, in the event the IRS says they didn't receive a return for a certain year, you'll be able to step in and set the record straight, saving time, money, and frustration.

Payroll records should be saved for quite some time as well; six years is recommended.

So where are you going to keep all these documents and how should they be filed? There are a multitude of different approaches you can take to filing. Many businesses set up a file for "Expenses/Vendors," "Sales/Invoices," and "Payroll" to start. You can organize each of these files alphabetically according to vendor, client, customer, or employee.

> *Note : Contracts with vendors, documents detailing commission structures, deeds and titles, property records, and partnership agreements, though they are not always directly relevant to your taxes, they should also be kept indefinitely. If you purchase property for your business and later sell it, you should keep your record of the property for three years after the year of the tax return on which the sale is reported.*

The Mileage Log

Mileage logs are often synonymous with small businesses, as most of them do need to use a vehicle for one reason or another and most are aware that mileage is a deductible expense. In 2015, the *standard mileage rate* is 57.5 cents per mile driven for business purposes. In 2014, that rate was 56 cents per mile. The mileage rate steadily increases year after year. Small business owners also have the albeit less popular option to not use the per-mile rate at all when calculating their car travel expenses. They may instead opt for the actual expense method, which requires the collection of all records that relate to the expense of maintaining and operating a vehicle for business purposes.

The *standard mileage rate* is meant to incorporate both the gas expense as well as the maintenance expense, depreciation, standard wear and tear and other associated vehicle expenses into one flat per-mile rate. If the business elects to use the standard mileage rate, the challenge is simple: keep track of all the miles traveled for business purposes. If 15,000 miles were used for business travel in 2015, then (15,000 * .575) or $8,625.00 would be the total deductible mileage expense. When using this method, you must also keep track of the date of the trip, the destination, and the business purpose. As a best practice, keep a log file in the vehicle that can be continually updated by any of the vehicle's users. If you or your employees are particularly tech savvy, then look into some mobile apps that can track and compile business mileage on your behalf.

> *Note : Your per mile rate subsumes all other expenses associated with your vehicle. If the vehicle requires a costly repair, that's not a deductible expense, nor are expenses for gas, insurance, or other incidental vehicle-related costs. These costs, however, are included in your deductions if you elect to use the "actual expense" method.*

In addition to the vehicle-related expenses already mentioned, if your business elects to use the ***actual expense method***, then you need to keep track of all vehicle lease payments, tires, registration fees, car washing expenses, tools you purchase to repair the vehicle, all parking expenses incurred during business trips, gas, oil, depreciation, and any other vehicle-related expenses directly related to the use of the vehicle for business purposes.

Ideally, the best way to determine which method you should use is to track all the required data for both methods and then simply use the one that one gives you the higher deduction. In practice, however, small business owners are more inclined to make an educated guess, and they can do so by keeping the following principles in mind:

If you end up on the fence with regard to which method to use for a new vehicle, then start off by using the standard mileage rate. If you use the actual expense method, then you are permanently prohibited from reverting back to the standard mileage rate for that vehicle for all forthcoming tax years. If you use the standard mileage rate for the first year that your business owns the vehicle, then you can switch to the actual expense method for a later year. Furthermore, you may even be able to switch back and forth, year-by-year if you use the standard rate for the vehicle's first year, though you will be subject to certain restrictions.

If you do want to do a side-by-side comparison of a vehicle expensed under the standard rate method and under the actual expense method, then the first year that the vehicle is used by the business is the ideal time to run the numbers. If you begin with year two, you have to at least wade through a couple of complicated restrictions before you can switch to a different method for any given vehicle.

Luxury vehicles, and most other higher-end vehicles, depreciate a lot more quickly than less expensive vehicles. Depreciation is a tax deductible expense. In fact, about 40% of the standard mileage rate is allocated for depreciation expense. If you have a less expensive vehicle, then you probably won't incur enough depreciation expense to surpass the 40% already accounted for in the standard mileage rate. Therefore, with less expensive vehicles, you're likely to do better using the standard mileage rate. If you rarely use your business vehicle, then you may be better off using the actual expense method. As a general rule, the more you drive, the less your cost per mile.

pop quiz

What Constitutes as Business Mileage & What Doesn't?

True or False : As a business owner, when you drive from your home to your office for your daily commute, you incur deductible mileage expense.

Answer : False, commuting is considered by the IRS to be a personal expense, and attempts to deduct commuting mileage frequently get people in trouble.

Here are the types of business trips that are deductible :

- *Errands* : When you go out to get printer ink, paper, or to restock on other supplies, the mileage is deductible. When you go to the bank or the post office to do a business-related task, the mileage is deductible. Using the vehicle to perform any errands for the business is always deductible.

- *Client Meetings* : If you're going to meet with a client or contractors at a location other than your standard place of business for the purpose of discussing business, then you're free to deduct the mileage it takes you to get there.

- *Temporary Job Sites* : If you're commuting to a location where your business is temporarily working, this location is known as a "temporary job site". So long as the work at the site isn't going to last any longer than one year, the commute from your home or primary job site to the temporary job site is deductible.

- *Driving to the Airport* : If you're taking a business trip by air and you drive to the airport, the expense is deductible.

- *Driving to a Secondary Office from your Home Office* : If you work from home, then you can greatly expand your total number of deductible miles, because you don't have to worry about trips that qualify as "commuting". Even if you have a separate office location, such as a co-op workspace, you may still deduct the mileage expenses from your home office to the secondary office.

Keep a Journal or Daily Planner

Face it, you're not always as meticulous as you should be, and sometimes you forget to enter in your mileage for a trip or file your expense record for your recent business purchase. One useful way to double check (and, when necessary, recreate) your records is by keeping a journal or daily planner with all your business activities. If your planner shows that you had a meeting with a client across town on February 8th, but you never recorded the mileage expense, then you can use Google maps to calculate the mileage required for the trip for deduction purposes. Having a detailed daily planner (and encouraging your employees to keep them as well) helps your business fill in the blanks before tax time. During audits, daily planners allow you to present verifiable data in the form of people and places. If need be, your claims can be validated by either the party with whom you met or by the venue.

Keep Accurate Financial Records

Even successful small businesses can get a little overwhelmed. When you're making a lot of sales and business is good, more work is required of you and your staff. You have to worry about replenishing inventories, hiring more employees, setting up new customers, and following up with customer needs. It's all too easy at times for good record keeping efforts to fall by the wayside. Failing to keep good financial records in the midst of a successful run can prove very problematic for a business in the longer term. It's more difficult to manage growth and cash flow when records aren't being maintained. It's also difficult to ensure that taxes are paid on time and that the amount paid is no less and no more than the amount owed.

Keeping current versions of the following financial reports:

- *Profit/Loss Statements* : Also known as "income statements," these statements are used to show the business's net profit. It does this essentially by summarizing the business's profits and expenses and subtracting the latter from the former. It's usually the net profit that's subject to being taxed.

- *Balance Sheets* : A statement that compares the sum of owner's equity and liabilities with the value of a business's assets. *Balance sheets* show the amount of payable taxes in relation to other liabilities owed by the business. A business that keeps good tabs on its tax accounts is more likely to be on top of its taxes and skates smoothly through an audit.

- *Copies of Previous Tax Returns* : If you've got your tax returns from previous years properly filed and organized, it is easy for auditors to trace your tax liability and payments from year to year. Though you're technically only obliged to keep your tax returns for 6 years, the best practice is to keep all of them forever in case the IRS claims you've failed to submit a return for a certain year.

- *Bank & Credit Card Statements* : If your bank account statements have no relevance to your business's taxes, then only save them for a year. If they are relevant to your business's taxes, then save them for seven years.

- *Checking Account Ledgers* : Hold onto these for seven years, along with your accounts receivable and accounts payable ledgers.

There's quite a lot to track in order to stay compliant. This is why 84% of small businesses use the services of a professional to keep their finances and taxes in order and for assistance in paying taxes and keeping track of them. The majority (55%) of those businesses reported that the latter obligation was the worse of the two burdens. Just 45% of those polled reported that actually paying the taxes was worse than having to keep track of them.

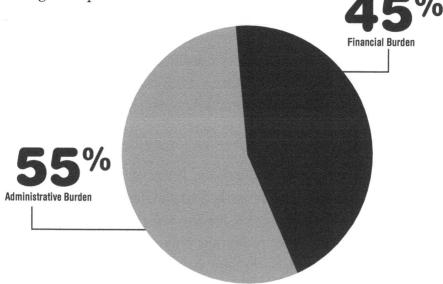

Fg. 1 : Cumulative burden by type imposed on small business by the Federal Tax Code

You should always be receptive to advice on how to improve the quality of your small business's record keeping.

Tricks of the trade that have been helpful to other small business owners:

Devote the Time

If you're handling the business's accounting and tax matters on your own, then be sure to devote a little bit of time each week (even if it's only 30 minutes) to record keeping tasks. You may not have enough time to get everything in perfect order, but it's much better to do a little at a time than to neglect your financial and tax paperwork over the long term. Financial and tax paperwork becomes more difficult to process the longer you wait to process it. It's easier to deal with financial and tax-relevant events from a few weeks ago than it is to deal with events from several months ago.

Devote the Tech

Especially if you're not going to hire a regular bookkeeper, you need to leverage technology in your pursuit of perfect records. Smaller businesses can often find decent accounting software at a lower rate. Research the possibilities and invest in one of these programs, then commit to its use.

Devote the Staff

Delegate record keeping duties to a competent member of your team whom you can trust, and ask that copies of the key reports mentioned in this chapter be submitted to you regularly.

Define Your Entity

Last, but probably foremost in importance, make sure your business is clearly defined. *Do not mix personal and business expenses!* You're setting yourself up for a record keeping nightmare. Refer back to Chapter 2 for information about choosing the optimal entity type for your business.

A Final Note About Records

Some business owners labor under the delusion that if they intentionally keep spotty records, then it is more difficult for IRS authorities to find anything incriminating during an audit. This is extremely dangerous thinking for few reasons. First, if you underestimate the IRS and they can find a way to show that you've intentionally obfuscated your records, then you could face serious tax penalties and even jail time. Second, an IRS audit is not like a criminal trial. They do not have to prove beyond a reasonable doubt that you owe more taxes than you've claimed to owe. You, not the IRS, bear the burden of proof. You must, therefore, provide thorough documentation showing— through the maintenance of excellent records!— that your assessment of your tax liability is accurate.

| 5 |

Handling Payroll Taxes

If you are confident that your payroll system is up and running correctly, you may want to skip the first part of this chapter. After reviewing the basics of setting up a payroll system for your business, we'll discuss the specific timelines that determine when your business's payroll taxes must be submitted. We'll also walk through the collection and submission of Federal Unemployment Tax.

Setting up your payroll correctly is a tedious process but well worth the time it takes to do it correctly. The first thing you need to do is obtain an employer tax ID number for your business, also known as an *employee identification number* or *EIN*. You use your EIN number when you file your federal and state taxes.

> *Note : You may also need to obtain specific ID numbers for your business from your state and local government. This text focuses primarily on your obligations under US federal law.*

Your employees must fill out a Federal Income Tax Withholding Form (W4), so that you know how much in taxes should be withheld from each employee's paycheck. You need to decide whether you want to process your payroll in-house, whether you want to invest in payroll processing software or do it by hand, or whether you want to assign the responsibility to an outside party. Regardless of which option you choose, you are still responsible for reporting and paying your payroll taxes. You also need to decide on the length of the pay period you wish to use; i.e. weekly, biweekly, or bimonthly.

If you're a new employer, then you need to pay, on a monthly or biweekly basis, the tax withholdings from your payroll in addition to your (the employer's) half of the Social Security and Medicare taxes. As of 2011, all federal tax deposits are to be made electronically. You may remit these payments through any of these four channels:

The *Electronic Federal Tax Payment System* – This is an online system that you can link to your bank account. Through this system, you may submit tax payments at any time either online or over the phone. In order to get set up with this system, you first have to apply for a pin number, which is sent to you in the mail. All that's left to do is to log in and link your bank account. If your business is new and you request an EIN number, then the IRS automatically enrolls you in the EFTPS system.

- *Direct ACH Payments* : You can initiate an ACH payment to the federal government directly from your bank account. Contact your bank to request this service.

- *Use Your Payroll Service Provider* : You can rely on your third-party payroll service to make the required payments for you.

- *Wire the Money* : You can always ask your bank to make a same-day wire payment to the fed, but you have to pay an unpleasant fee. So, this option might be best as a last resort.

If your employment taxes total to less than $2,500 per quarter, then you may submit the taxes with your quarterly *estimated tax* payments. If your business's employment taxes are greater than $2,500 for the quarter, then you need to submit your taxes either on a monthly or on a biweekly basis.

To determine whether you need to submit on a monthly or biweekly basis, you need to understand the concept of a *lookback period.*

A lookback period refers to the four quarters culminating on June 30th of the previous year. If your business deposited $50,000 or less during the course of your current lookback period, then you are only required to deposit your taxes on a monthly basis. If you deposited over $50,000 during the course of your lookback period, then you need to deposit on a biweekly basis. Let's say, for example, that it's May of 2015 and you run a toy store. You have recently downsized significantly to the point at which you're no longer generating more than $2,500 per quarter in payroll taxes. Since it's 2015, your lookback period includes the four quarters terminating on June 30th of 2014 (July 1st 2013 through June 30th 2014). Even though you're now a much smaller business than you were, during the lookback period you deposited a total of $54,000 dollars in payroll tax. Therefore, you must deposit your payroll tax on a biweekly basis.

Note : If the business has just opened, or has just begun collecting payroll tax, then the lookback period has a value of zero and the business must deposit payroll taxes on a monthly basis.

Now, let's say that your toy store has three employees and that you pay your employees twice a month, on the 15th and on the last day of the month (30th/31st). It's still May 2015, and you've withheld (and paid taxes) on the 15th and the 31st. Now, for the sake of argument, assume that your toy store *did not* meet its $50,000 lookback period threshold, and you're only responsible for depositing taxes monthly. Your May taxes are due no later than the 15th day of June.

Companies required to deposit payroll taxes on a monthly basis must do so by the 15th day of the following month. If you revert to the reality in which the lookback period for your toy store does exceed the $50,000 threshold, then you are required to deposit your tax withholdings (plus payments) on a biweekly basis. Here's what that looks like: say your payday is on a Friday. The payroll taxes have to be deposited by the following Wednesday. The same Wednesday due date applies if the payday was on a Thursday or a Wednesday. Hence, you'll have between five and seven days to deposit your tax withholdings (and payments). If your payday is on a Saturday, Sunday, Monday or Tuesday, then the deposits are due by the following Friday (three to six days after the payday). Under no circumstances should you have fewer than three business days to deposit your taxes.

Note : If there's any confusion as to the difference between business <u>withholding taxes</u> and <u>paying taxes</u>, then let's clear it up now. Withholding taxes refers to amounts deducted from the employees' salaries or wages, while paying taxes refers to the business's payment of its share of the employee's Social Security and Medicare tax. Each of these tax liabilities is split evenly between employee and employer.

Note : Staying true to the assumption that a business never has less than three business days to make its tax deposit: if there is a legal holiday that prevents you from getting your three business day window, then your tax due date is bumped back by a day. For example, if you pay your employees on a Friday and Monday is a legal holiday, then your deposits are due on Thursday as opposed to Wednesday in accordance with the three business day minimum.

If you end up submitting a deposit that's less than the required amount for the period, then you may be fined unless the amount by which you're short fails to exceed $100 or 2% of your required amount.

To illustrate, here's an example :

A business owner withholds (and pays) a total of $20,000 in payroll tax and is required to pay that amount by Wednesday of the following week. His administrative assistant makes an error and deposits $19,600 rather than $20,000. Is the business subject to a penalty for failing to deposit the proper amount?

Answer : The business is not immediately subject to a penalty. Since the deposit was short by $400, which is exactly two percent of the required deposit, no penalty is assessed on the spot.

When, as in the example, a business is short on its tax deposit, it is given a specific allotment of time to pay the shortage. If the business is depositing on a monthly basis, then it has until the next quarterly filing due date to make the necessary correction. If the business is filing biweekly, then it needs to account for the correction by the 15th day of the month following the month on which the shortfall occurred. If the due date for the quarterly return is going to come before the 15th of the following month, then the shortfall must be reconciled by the due date.

Federal Unemployment Tax

Federal unemployment tax, often referred to as *FUTA* tax, is based on the *Federal Unemployment Tax Act*, which compensates workers who've lost their jobs. Most employers pay an unemployment tax to their state as well as to the federal government.

If your business paid $1500 or more in wages during the course of any calendar quarter in the current or immediately previous year, then you must pay unemployment taxes. The amount of unemployment tax paid by various employers depends greatly on the state in which the employer operates. The federal unemployment tax rate begins at 6%, but this rate can be reduced by credits that go into effect when a state levies its own unemployment taxes. The maximum credit receivable is 5.4%, so the minimum FUTA rate is .6%. Not every business in a given state is subject to the same credit amount. New businesses, for example, may be subject to more of a credit than businesses that have been in operation for a while. Every state has a specific rate to which new employers are subject.

FUTA taxes are paid on the basis of a wage base for each employee. The employer must continue to pay FUTA taxes on an employee's wages until the employee's year-to-date wages exceed $7000; after that point, no FUTA taxes are assessed *on that employee* until the next year. Since $7000 is the maximum amount of wages that can be taxed, the maximum amount collected for each employee is $420, or $7000 x .06. The minimum amount that can be collected for an employee is $42.

The IRS operates under the assumption that your business is paying state unemployment tax of 5.6% and thus owes the Fed .06%. The IRS thus requires the submission of FUTA taxes (equal to .06% of your eligible payroll) by the end of the month following the last month of your business quarter. For example, all the FUTA taxes you collect in April through June must be remitted to the IRS by July 31st.

What if I Don't Pay My Payroll Taxes?

Let's assume you've got a small business that's generating a considerable number of sales, but also has a lot of expenses, employees, utilities, inventory and so forth. You find that pretty much all the cash you're taking in is going straight back out just to keep up with bare necessities of running your business. Perhaps you've not budgeted carefully enough for your tax liability. Or maybe some of the clients you've been servicing have been paying their bills late. You continue to withhold payroll taxes from your employees, but you don't make your required deposits on time.

Payroll taxes are one area in which the repercussions from the IRS come very swiftly. They view payroll withholdings as, by all rights, their money, part of a specific trust fund that they own.

Note : The IRS considers the money withheld from employees to be theirs and temporarily held "in trust" by the employer. This is why a violation of the arrangement is met with such viciousness from the IRS. They view it as a violation of an important trust.

One thing that separates the payroll taxes your business owes from other taxes is that past due payroll taxes are viewed as a personal liability. Even if your business is set up as a limited liability company or a corporation—these entities theoretically protect the owner(s) from personal liability—the IRS can still take your car, your house, or other assets for failure to submit your payroll taxes.

There's a dreaded penalty known as the *Trust Fund Recovery Penalty (TFRP)* or the "100 Percent Penalty" that's levied against business owners or officers who fail to pay their payroll taxes. This penalty entails the obligation to pay double the amount of payroll taxes that you'd have had to pay had you paid them on time. Again, this penalty has a personal reach and can be levied against a bookkeeper, a CFO, virtually any person responsible for withholding and submitting payroll taxes. One way you can avoid this responsibility is by hiring a third party payroll service provider to run your payroll. Assuming you don't instruct them to violate payroll withholding requirements, they are responsible for withholding and depositing the proper amounts on your behalf.

In the event you or someone in your organization is found to be responsible for not withholding or remitting payroll tax, you will receive a letter from the IRS stating their plans to levy the TFRP penalty against you.

Independent Contractors vs. Employees

Many businesses strongly prefer to hire contractors rather than employees because the tax burden is relatively miniscule. When a business hires an independent contractor, it does not pay any share of the contractor's Social Security or Medicare taxes. The contractor is responsible for the entirety of these taxes. The IRS strongly prefers businesses that hire employees rather than contractors whenever there's any ambiguity, because with employees, it's easier for the IRS to collect its money. Contractors are responsible for paying their own taxes. When a business pays a contractor, nothing is withheld.

Recently, the IRS has implemented new punitive measures for businesses that erroneously hire contract labor when they technically should be hiring employee labor. In a 2010 court case, *United States vs.*

Hudson, the IRS went after a real estate management company that was hiring contract laborers who, in the opinion of the IRS, should have been hired as employees. The IRS won the court case and the real estate management company was then forced to pay the payroll taxes it would have been paying had the contract laborers been classified correctly. The effects of the lost law suit were so financially devastating that the real estate management company ended up declaring bankruptcy.

Reporting Obligations

Certain tax documents must be submitted to both employees and independent contractors hired by your business during the course of a given year. The basic information conveyed by these tax documents is quite simple: they show how much taxable income the employee or contractor earned thanks to employment by your business, and they also show how much money, if any, was withheld for taxes.

Employees receive a W-2 "Wage and Tax Statement" form for the calendar year. These forms must be issued by the 31st of January on the following year. So for example, 2014 W-2s were issued by employers no later than January 31st 2015.

Under some circumstances, W-2s must be delivered early. Sometimes, however, they cannot be delivered at all because the intended recipient can't be located. These scenarios arise when an employee separates from your company during a given calendar year. Employees that are terminated may request that they receive their W-2s earlier than the January 31st deadline. If such a request is made, then you must honor it within 30 days from the date of request or 30 days from the date that the last paycheck to the terminated employee was issued. If no request is made, then you send out the terminated employee's W-2 along with the rest of them before the January 31st due date. Use the address you have on file for the terminated employee. If the employee is no longer at that address, and he doesn't contact your business to update his records, then you should retain and file the undeliverable W-2.

Note : You must also submit a copy of your employees' W2s to the SSA (Social Security Administration) by the end of February or by April 1st if you're filing electronically.

For independent contractors, you do not send and file a W-2, but a 1099-Misc. The deadlines are essentially the same. You must send the contractor her 1099-Misc by January 31st, and then send the IRS its copy by the end of February.

Note : Depending in which state your business operates, you may also be required to issue additional informative documents for your employees and contractors as well as notices to the state government or tax authority. Intuit, the company behind the famous QuickBooks software, has published a helpful article showing a chart of which states require which documents: http://payroll.intuit.com/support/kb/2000524.html

As a final note, remember to keep copies of your payroll records for six years. These should include records of your withholdings and deposits. Keep these records organized and prepared for an audit, as the IRS reserves the right to inspect these records at any time.

| 6 |
The Most Important Deductions

It's difficult running a small business. Not only do you not have access to the powerful, scalable resources and deep cash reserves of larger businesses, but you also face a peculiar, complicated, and rigorous tax scenario.

As we mentioned in the introduction of this book, it usually takes three to four months before small businesses reach a point at which the money they earn won't be going just to pay their taxes. Over the past few decades, lawmakers, along with advocacy committees and associations, have recognized the plight of small businesses and have done what they could to provide avenues for relief. This chapter showcases the *tax deductions* and exemptions for which your small business may qualify.

The Home Office Deduction

Many self-employed individuals and small businesses that use a portion of their homes for business purposes have been spooked by claims that taking the home office deduction is a surefire way to procure a visit from the IRS. In truth, this deduction can be capitalized upon accurately and safely, and can save you a good amount of money.

To take the home office deduction correctly, the first thing you must do is ensure that the space you want to claim is used both *regularly and exclusively* for the purposes of running your business[8]. Just recently (2013) the IRS introduced a new, simpler way of claiming your home office deduction using a standard rate of $5 per square foot for the area that's used for your home office. Similar to the mileage deduction, the taxpayer has the option to either use the standard rate ($5) or to calculate the actual expense of the home office itself. To do this you'd first need to determine the square footage of the home office area, then express it as a percentage of the entire home. For instance, if you have a home office that's 500 square feet and your entire home is 2500 square feet, then 20% of your home is being used for your home office. From here, you'd take 20% of your rent, mortgage, utilities, and your homeowner's insurance and use this to total your home office exemption. Or, you could simply multiply 500 by $5 and determine that you have an exemption worth $2500.

> *Note : Your home office does not have to constitute an entire room in your home, but can be a part of a room. It helps to have some clear divider, like a book case or a desk that clearly separates the office part of the room devoted to the business from the rest of the room.*

The Pros & Cons of Working from Home

Everyone needs a space from which to run a company, be it a tiny desk in your basement, a bigger desk in an office complex, space in a huge corporate center, or a store in the neighborhood shopping mall. Where you choose to work has a huge impact on your tax deductions so, if you're currently in the thinking stage and not sure whether or not to make your home your office, the information below offers you some food for thought.

Rules & Regulations

If a home-based business sounds like a good idea to you, your local municipality may feel differently. A lot of local governments have very specific rules about who can operate a home business, how, and where. That means it's important to be in contact with someone from your local government office who knows the ins and outs of home businesses in your municipality.

You'll need the answers to some important questions, such as:

- What permits (if any) are necessary to operate a home business?

- Are employees permitted to work with you and how many?

- Are customers permitted to come to your home? Is there a limit as to how many people or vehicles are permitted at any one time? Will you need to provide additional parking?

- Are there restrictions on outside signage?

- Can you make physical changes to your home to accommodate conducting business?

The answers to these questions are essential to your decision of whether or not to move forward with your home business plan. If you're satisfied that the regulations will not be a hindrance, you can then proceed to other considerations.

Cost Effectiveness

In most cases, choosing a home-based business is very wise in regards to keeping down your costs. Truly, a business operated out of your home is essentially rent-free. You won't be saddled with an additional monthly bill for renting costly space elsewhere. In addition, you can enjoy the tax write-offs associated with operating from your home, even if you're only using a small portion of your home. There are a few different ways to file returns for home office deductions – a simplified version and another that's not so simple – but with a little research and perhaps a chat with someone experienced in small businesses taxes – you can determine which one is right for you.

However, don't get caught up in the idea that everything you do inside your home is deductible. Again, there are very specific rules and you may *only* deduct expenses *directly* to operating your business.

Life Gets in the Way

While it's generally a wise and cost-effective idea to operate your business from your home when possible, there are those who just don't fare well when they are distracted by the everyday goings-on of home life. If you don't feel as if you have the discipline to get down to work when the kids are fussing or that broken sink is calling your name or your favorite TV show is on, then working from home may not be a wise idea. Or perhaps the space you're considering really doesn't provide you with enough privacy or peace and quiet to accomplish your daily work-related tasks. Then you may have to reconsider.

On the positive side, many parents find that running a home-based business gives them the flexibility to be there when their children need them. For many, this is a prime consideration for choosing to work from home.

Conversely, some individuals who operate their businesses from home seem to have a hard time ending the business day and moving on to enjoying some personal time, be it alone or with their families. If your business is in your house, it's often too easy to return to the office after dinner or late at night, something you probably wouldn't do if you had to get in your car and drive to your office. Hence, you may find that a home business greatly interferes with your family life or downtime. If that's the case, it may not be right for you.

Business-Related Meals & Entertainment

This one's not nearly as difficult to track as people think. If you're out with a customer or a prospective customer—whether it's at a restaurant, a bar, a football game, or a Broadway show—and you end up paying for the food and entertainment, you can write off 50% of your expense as an entertainment expense. In order to qualify, the meeting must be related directly to business activity and business matters must be discussed at the event. The entertainment element of the event must transpire before or after relevant business discussion. To keep your meals and entertainment expenses above-boards and audit-friendly, make sure to keep all of your receipts and to notate the business matter discussed and parties involved on that receipt.

Travel Expenses

Travel Within the US

When you're traveling inside the country, you can deduct most expenses associated with travel (a few rules do apply) such as your airfare, your rental car, the cost of your hotel, sending faxes, and taxis. It doesn't matter whether you choose shabby accommodations at the Motel 6 or the Grand Hyatt, the IRS views these as deductible expenses. The only thing you must be mindful of here is the extent to which your travels involve business activity. You're required to carefully distinguish between genuine business activities (and the associated expenses) and personal expenses, such as sight-seeing or visiting family or friends. *Transportation costs*, such as taxis, airfare, and bus fare are fully deductible if you spend at least half of your time on business matters. Transportation costs are different from "destination costs," which include expenses that occur once you arrive at your destination, such as food, hotel, and local transportation, including public transportation or rental vehicles. Your destination costs may only be deducted on days on which you engage in business activity. On days on which you do not conduct business, you must pay all of your ***destination expenses*** personally.

You may bring your spouse, children, or friends along with you on a business trip, but their expenses may not be deducted unless they are both employees of the company and accompanying you for business purposes.

Note : It's generally thought that so long as your traveling partner does not add any incremental expenses to what would have otherwise been spent, then you can write off the entirety of certain expenses, such as hotel rooms or cab rides for which no fees are charged for additional riders. Always run the test, though, and ask yourself if you're spending more than you'd otherwise be spending due to the accompaniment of your traveling companion. If you are spending more, then that extra expenditure may not be deducted.

Travel Outside the US

Things get a little more complicated when it comes to traveling outside the US for business. If your trip is longer than seven days and you spend less than 50% of your time working, then you may not deduct any of your expenses for the duration of the trip. If you spend between 50% and 75% of your long trip working, then you need to note that percentage and apply it to your transportation costs. For example, if you spend $10,000 on transportation costs and worked 60% of the time, then you can deduct only $6,000. You're still able to deduct destination costs, but only on the days that you spend working. If you spend more than 75% of your long trip (longer than seven days) working, then you can deduct 100% of your transportation costs along with the destination costs on the days you spend working. If the duration of your trip is shorter than seven days, the same rules apply. All of your transportations costs are deductible along with destination costs for the days you work.

Note : This breakdown of travel expenses is a summary-level breakdown. To view the highly detailed, specific IRS rules governing travel, entertainment, and other expenses, see IRS Publication 463: Travel, Entertainment, Gift, and Car Expenses : http://www.irs.gov/pub/irs-pdf/p463.pdf.

Section 179 Deductions

The beginning of this chapter mentioned that some lawmakers have attempted to make life a little easier for small business owners by passing key pieces of legislation. The **Section 179 tax deduction** is one of these key pieces of legislation.

Usually, when a business purchases a piece of equipment, the business is able to write off the expense of that equipment bit by bit in the form of depreciation—the amount of resale value that the equipment loses over time. The purpose of Section 179 is to encourage businesses to spend more on equipment while they can write off the entire cost. The theory is that if businesses were considering new equipment purchases, then they would be more inclined to do so while Section 179 was still in effect with a high maximum deduction. The maximum deduction from 2010 through 2014 was $500,000. The regular maximum deduction—before 2010 and after 2014—was only $25,000. The purpose of increasing the maximum allowable deduction was to get businesses to jump at the opportunity to invest in new equipment and hopefully spur on the whole economy.

Section 179 is thought to be one of the few components of recent economic stimulus measures that were actually aimed at helping smaller businesses. Unfortunately, for the present day tax payer, the special $500,000 limit has yet to be renewed, so as of 2015 only equipment expenses of up to $25,000 may be deducted. The Section 179 deduction applies to businesses purchasing equipment regardless if they choose to purchase the equipment outright, on a lease, or via financing.

Deducting Self-Employment Tax

For small businesses and self-employed individuals, the employer-equivalent portion of the self-employment tax may be deducted when your gross income is figured. This deduction only affects your income tax liability. It does not change your net profit or loss, nor does it affect the total amount of self-employment tax that you owe.

Deducting the Cost of Health Insurance Premiums

In accordance with the Small Business Jobs Act, signed into law in 2010, self-employed individuals and small business owners may deduct their health insurance premiums. This deduction is figured into the business's net earnings, reducing its income tax liability. You do not qualify for this deduction if you are eligible to be covered under your spouse's insurance plan. Conversely, if your spouse worked for your small business in a real capacity (not just for paperwork purposes), then her insurance premiums are fully deductible. If your children depend on you for health coverage, then their premiums are also deductible expenses.

Interest Expenses

If you're doing what you should be doing, and keeping your business expenses separate from your personal expenses, then you can easily deduct any interest charges incurred by credit cards used for business purposes. The same applies to interest owed on loans from a bank or elsewhere. Just be sure to keep clear records showing that the money gained was used to support the business.

Software Expenses

Let's say you decide to purchase the latest tax software from Intuit. Theoretically, computer software shouldn't be deducted outright but depreciated over a 36-month period of time. However, thanks to the Section 179 deduction, if your software was used in the service of your business at any time from January 1, 2003 to December 31, 2014, then you are eligible to write off the entire cost of software in the year that it was purchased, so long as the total cost of the software was within the prescribed Section 179 maximum deductible amounts. If you purchased the software in 2015, then you can still deduct the entire price of the software (up to $25,000) under the Section 179 exemption, so long as you begin using the software by the end of the day on December 31, 2015. If your software purchase exceeds the allowable Section 179 deduction, then the amount spent in excess of $25,000 must be capitalized and will be depreciated over three years (36 months).

Note : With the advent of Quickbooks Online and multiple other wholly cloud-based software-as-a-service (SAAS) technologies, off-the-shelf software may not be as standard. If you're using a cloud-based software solution with a monthly subscription, then it's ok to deduct your subscription cost in full as an Office Expense.

Family Employees

Many small business owners like to get the whole family involved in the work at-hand. One of the perks of working as a family is that it opens up your business to a handful of tax advantages. For starters, the wages or salary you pay to a family member can be deducted from your taxable business income, provided that the amount paid is a "reasonable amount" commensurate with the job being performed. The IRS won't let things slide here. If you're paying a family member a wage or salary that doesn't reflect the market rate, then you're asking for trouble.

In some states, if you hire your son or daughter, you do not have to pay for his or her Social Security Tax, Medicare Tax, or FUTA taxes. The extent to which you can take advantage of these breaks depends on the state and the age of the child, but generally, if the child you hire is younger than 21, then you do not have to pay FUTA tax until the child turns 21. If the child is younger than 18, you don't have to pay Social Security and Medicare tax until the child turns 18.

Note : These family-based tax exemptions are most common in sole proprietorships. In a corporation or partnership, these rules do not apply unless all shareholders or partners are parents of the child.

If you employ your spouse, then your spouse's income is subject to Social Security and Medicare withholdings, but not FUTA taxes.

Retirement Contributions

If you're a young person who's decided to tackle owning your own business, chances are you're thinking little about retirement. Truly, even older Americans – both those who are self-employed or who work for others - may not take the time to think about planning for the future. After all, spending is fun and immediate rewards are exciting. However, in this age of dwindling pensions and iffy Social Security promises, saving for retirement is more important than ever. In addition, there are a number of reasons why small business owners need to consider investing in retirement accounts for themselves and for their employees.

Tax Breaks

"Retirement accounts really should be called tax-reduction accounts," says personal finance expert, Eric Tyson. "If they were, people might be more eager to contribute to them." Indeed, opening and contributing to any kind of retirement account will help you reduce your tax bill. The upfront breaks are obvious. If you're being taxed at 30 percent, for example, and you contribute $5,000 a year to a retirement fund, you trim $1500 a year off your tax bill. Lower income earners may receive even more perks for their contributions.

But there are ongoing tax advantages as well. As your retirement account grows via interest, dividends, and appreciation, you gain all that money without being taxed on it. Taxes on this accumulating money are deferred until you withdraw it sometime later in life. For many, that is a twice-win situation as their tax bracket is lower during retirement.

How Much Should I Save?

Before deciding what kind of retirement vehicle you should choose for your investment and that of your employees, think about how much you'll need to save. Financial experts agree that the retired individual generally needs about 70 to 80 percent of his pre-retirement income to thrive during retirement in the same manner to which he is accustomed. So, if you earn $100,000 per year, this estimate says you'll need $70-80,000 annually in retirement to maintain your lifestyle. Therefore, your investment counselor can help you choose a retirement account to put you at that level after you've stopped working. Of course, the earlier you begin to save, the better.

Choosing the Right Retirement Accounts for a Small Business

It's important to know that if you, the business owner, are making contributions to a retirement account for yourself, you are required to make comparable contributions to accounts set up for your employees. However, this is nothing from which to shy away. If you understand this from the beginning, you can figure these contributions into the employee's entire salary package.

Once you understand the rules, it's time to set about making the correct choices for you and your employees. There are many types of accounts to choose from, and the size of your business and number of employees will help determine and influence your choices.

- **SEP-IRA** : A "simplified employee pension individual retirement account" – or SEP-IRA – is the simplest form of retirement savings. You decide how much you want to contribute (there are no minimums but there are maximum contributions) and you don't even have to file any paperwork with the IRS. Furthermore, it's quite easy to set these up for you and your employees.

- **Keogh plans** : A little more complex, Keogh plans have the same contribution parameters as IRAs, but you have to do more administrative work, including filing an annual Form 5500 with the IRS. Advantages include the fact that Keoghs allow vesting schedules, which means that an employee can be required to work for the company for a specified number of years before she earns the right to her full account balance. You can decide at what point an employee becomes fully-vested and has access to 100% of her Keogh plan. In addition, the Keogh allows for Social Security integration, which means that higher-earning employees can receive larger percentage contributions to their accounts. This is advantageous because Social Security taxes top out after an individual earns a certain amount (which changes from year to year), and this integration enables business owners and top employees who earn in excess of this amount to make up for this cap.

- **SIMPLE plans** : Using a SIMPLE (savings incentive match plans for employees) IRA, employers make contributions to these funds on behalf of employees, either matching dollar for dollar the first 3 percent the employee contributes or contributing 2 percent of the pay for everyone whose salary exceeds $5,000. Some opponents of these plans note that the first contribution schedule gives employers a reason not to educate their employees about the advantages of saving for retirement.

- **401(k) plans** : These are best suited to larger small businesses and are among the most common retirement plans offered. In 2016, $18,000 is the maximum contribution an employee under age 50 can make to his 401(k). Those over 50 can contribute as much as $6,000 more. Contributions are excluded from your income and are free from taxes at the federal level (and often at the state level as well). Employers may contribute as well. You'll need to consult with a mutual fund or discount brokerage organization to set up 401(k) accounts.

Every Deduction Under the Sun

With a tax code as complex and lengthy as the one we use in the US (not to mention all of the state-based add-ons), an entire catalog of all available tax deductions is encyclopedic in scale. These are a few examples of certain deductions or credits that may have flown under your radar. For a more complete listing, and even a specialized list of some exceptionally strange tax deductions, check out the Loophole Lewy website for small businesses.

At the end of this book, just before the Glossary of Terms, is a 10-question deduction quiz that will help you drill and apply your knowledge of the tax deductions described in this chapter.

| 7 |

Common Business Tax Mistakes

Reading and adhering to the suggestions in this chapter can make it a little more difficult for the IRS to find fault with your business. They're used to seeing the same mistakes over and over again. If you can narrow down some of these common tax pitfalls, your return is unlikely to get flagged because of them.

Receipts Aren't Enough

No doubt you've heard the stories of business owners walking into their accountant's offices with boxes full of receipts and nothing else. It's a tax professional's nightmare and a scenario that's just not fair to your hired tax help. Instead of just throwing receipts in a folder and thinking someone else will sort them, keep a tax diary or – at the very least – write specific details on each receipt and file them in individual folders according to category. Then ask your tax expert how to best present them.

Don't Borrow from Designated Tax Accounts

Can't pay your bills this month? Need to get creative to make ends meet? Well, don't borrow money from the trust fund that's earmarked for employee withholding! This is not only wrong and a bad business practice but it could get you into heaps of trouble with the Feds as well.

Don't Celebrate your Tax Refund

If, at the end of the tax year, you're entitled to a huge refund, don't see it as "extra" money. The fact that you're getting lots of money back means you grossly overpaid. The government just used a whole lot of your money for free! You obviously need to meet with your tax folks to decide on some adjustments so that you're not paying too much on a regular basis.

Don't Take Too Much Salary from the Business

Certainly you'll want to pay yourself, especially as your business grows, but be sure it is reasonable for the amount you take in on an annual basis. For example, if you pay yourself $50,000 one year and then triple it the following year, despite fairly stagnate profits, red flags will go up at the IRS and you may be charged with taking unreasonable compensation.

Get the Retirement Plans Up & Running

Our tendency to put our retirement savings on the back burner seems to also extend into our lives as entrepreneurs. Too many business owners drag their feet when setting up retirement accounts for themselves and for their employees. Many of them don't realize that they can deduct their personal retirement contributions, as well as any contributions made to their employees' retirement plans. It doesn't matter which entity you choose; you can still set up a broad range of plans through your business including:

- 401(k) plans
- Roth 401(k) plans
- SIMPLE
- SEP

Stay in Regular Touch with your Accountant

Inc.com reports that about 18 percent of all small business owners only talk to their accountants during tax time. That's not wise! You should be seeking advice from your tax professional year-round, including instructions for payment of quarterly estimated taxes and other obligations that might exist throughout the year. Consider keeping him on a retainer or negotiating an affordable per hour price for his services.

Know When to Call it Quits

If you've reached year three or four and your business is still losing money, it's time to examine whether or not you really have a business. Also note that you're not the only one noticing the consistent losses. The IRS has its eye on you, too, and may start to disallow your losses, deciding that your business really isn't a business at all but perhaps a just a costly and time-consuming hobby.

conclusion

An overview of the U.S. tax particulars for small businesses, such as this book, is just that…an overview. Because there are so many levels of taxation – federal, state, county, city – and so many different rules that apply to each, it can certainly seem like you're never completely sure that what you're doing to keep up with your tax liability is correct.

However, if you become a student of "Small Business Taxes 101" and make it a point to stay abreast of all the current laws, you'll do fine. That means carving time out of your week – or even month – to review what's new as far as taxes are concerned. It might also mean an extra meeting with your tax professional or a little more time spent pouring over your tax software program, which should be updated annually. It might involve extra paperwork or a few additional minutes spent with that mileage ledger. But that's all time well spent as you'll emerge with a better understanding of your tax liability and a slimmer chance that you'll be audited by the IRS.

So, in short… plan, plan, and plan some more! Know what you owe and don't allow yourself to come up short. Understand that taxes – and paying them – are a huge part of owning and running a business. Never allow yourself to get buried in confusion, and don't let fear get in your way. Most of all, be open to reaching out for help. That's why accountants and bookkeepers were put on this earth!

bonus quiz

Answers begin on page 70

1. You rent a studio apartment and use a particular section of the apartment regularly and exclusively to run your drop shipping business. The total amount of square footage you use to run your business is 30 square feet in area, and you wish to use the standard deduction. Is this a deductible expense?

2. You have a room in your home that's 50 square-feet in area. You occasionally use the computer in the room to answer business-related emails, but normally your wife uses the room for sewing. The room represents about 15% of your entire home's square footage. Can you deduct 15% of your mortgage, your utilities, and your home owner's insurance premium using the home office credit?

3. Since your small business courts clients from all over the country, you and your partners spend a lot of money on airfare. You decided to get a business credit card from American Express with good frequent flyer benefits. Unfortunately, last month you were assessed $250 in interest payments. Is this a deductible expense?

4. You purchase an off-the-shelf propriety software product in April of 2015 and begin using it the same day. The software is a special, limited-edition, business-class social media monitoring software from Radian 6 Technologies and is priced at $30,000. Is this a deductible expense for 2015? How much of the expense is immediately deductible?

5. Your business has purchased a new economy vehicle for business travel. You use the vehicle to travel 20 miles to a temporary job site that will be active for four months and wish to use the vehicle to take the standard mileage exemption of 57.5 cents. Is this a deductible expense?

6. A former college friend of yours is in town for the weekend and the two of you hit up the local sports bar to watch your alma mater compete in a collegiate football game. The two of you exchange stories about your different jobs and you ask for career advice. Is your bar tab of $27.50 a deductible expense?

7. A new client requests that you meet him at his office to discuss a business-related matter. You leave your home in the morning and drive 15 miles, straight to his office, for a meeting. Is your mileage deductible?

8. You're CEO of a growing business, and you're thinking about taking your company public. You travel to New York City to meet with an attorney who has expertise in taking privately owned businesses public. You stay in New York for three days and meet with the attorney only on day 1. On days 2 & 3 you

spend $1000 on meals and hotels. Are your meals and hotel expenses (destination expenses) deductible on days 2 & 3?

9. Your wife accompanies you on a business trip to Dallas, Texas. She regularly assists you with data-entry projects, and she drives the rental car for you so you can look over briefs. Her meal expenses for the trip total $500. Your wife is not an employee of the company. Is this $500 amount deductible as a business expense?

10. You're attending a conference in Germany related to your auto parts business. You've made arrangements to spend two full weeks (14 days) in Germany. The conference lasts five days and commences the day after you arrive in Germany. The conference ends and you arrange to meet privately (for business purposes) with two individuals whom you met at the conference. You meet with these individuals one at a time on two separate days during your final week in Germany. The total cost of your airfare, along with other transportation costs, was $1200. You spent a total of $2500 in destination costs during the course of the conference, and you spent a total of $200 during your meetings with the people you met at the conference. Based on this data, how much in expenses can you write off?

1. Answer : It's a deductible expense since the section of the apartment in question is used exclusively and regularly for business. The total deduction is $150 (30sqft * $5).

Table 1

Expense #	Expense Type	Expense Amount	Deductible (y/n)	Notes
1	Home Office	$ 150.00	Yes	30 sq. ft. * 5
2				
3				

2. Answer : You may neither deduct 15% of the "actual" expenses nor deduct $5 for each square foot of the room. The room does not qualify for the home office exemption because it is not used regularly and exclusively for your business.

3. Answer : Your interest expense is fully deductible because the credit account that incurred the interest is used exclusively for business purposes.

Table 2

Expense #	Expense Type	Expense Amount	Deductible (y/n)	Notes
1	Home Office	$ 150.00	Yes	30 sq. ft. * 5
2	Home Office	N/A	No	
3	Interest Payments	$ 250.00	Yes	

4. Answer : Since you began using the product during the 2015 calendar year, the expense is fully deductible up to $25,000 per the Section 179 exemption on record for 2015. The remaining $5000 is subject to the standard rules that govern off-the-shelf software purchases. The $5000 must be capitalized and it is allowed to depreciate over three years' time.

Table 3

Expense #	Expense Type	Expense Amount	Deductible (y/n)	Notes
1	Home Office	$ 150.00	Yes	30 sq. ft. * 5
2	Home Office	N/A	No	
3	Interest Payments	$ 250.00	Yes	
4	Software	$ 25,000.00	Yes	25 of 30K immediately deductible
	Depreciation (yr 1)	$1,667.00	Yes	1/3 of Remaining 5K
	Depreciation (yr 2)	$1,667.00	Yes	1/3 of Remaining 5K
	Depreciation (yr 3)	$1,667.00	Yes	1/3 of Remaining 5K

5. *Answer* : This is a deductible expense, because you are not using the vehicle to commute to or from work, but to a separate business site that will not be active for longer than a year (at which point it's considered to be a "permanent job site" and travel will not be deductible).

Table 4

Expense #	Expense Type	Expense Amount	Deductible (y/n)	Notes
1	Home Office	$ 150.00	Yes	30 sq. ft. * 5
2	Home Office	N/A	No	
3	Interest Payments	$ 250.00	Yes	
4	Software	$ 25,000.00	Yes	25 of 30K immediately deductible
	Depreciation (yr 1)	$1,667.00	Yes	1/3 of Remaining 5K
	Depreciation (yr 2)	$1,667.00	Yes	1/3 of Remaining 5K
	Depreciation (yr 3)	$1,667.00	Yes	1/3 of Remaining 5K
5	Mileage	$ 11.50	Yes	20 mi * 57.5 cents

6. Answer : Your bar tab is not a deductible expense. The meeting was set up for the express and personal purpose of reconnecting with an old friend. Even though you discussed your career, this does not constitute a business meeting.

7. Answer : Your mileage expense is deductible, because traveling to your client's office is not a part of your regular commute.

Table 5

Expense #	Expense Type	Expense Amount	Deductible (y/n)	Notes
4	Software	$ 25,000.00	Yes	25 of 30K immediately deductible
	Depreciation (yr 1)	$1,667.00	Yes	1/3 of Remaining 5K
	Depreciation (yr 2)	$1,667.00	Yes	1/3 of Remaining 5K
	Depreciation (yr 3)	$1,667.00	Yes	1/3 of Remaining 5K
5	Mileage	$ 11.50	Yes	20 mi * 57.5 cents
6	Bar Tab	N/A	No	
7	Mileage	$ 8.63	Yes	15 mi * 57.5 cents

8. Answer : Meals and hotels constitute "destination costs" and are hence only deductible on days during which business is conducted. Because you only conducted business on day one, the destination costs from days two and three are not deductible.

9. Answer : Even though your wife is helping you by performing business tasks, her expenses are not deductible. In order for the expenses of a traveling companion to be deductible, she must be both on the trip for business purposes and an employee of the company.

10. Answer : Since the total duration of your trip in Germany is 14 days and you spent five days at the conference and had business meetings on two other days, then you've used a total of seven days out of the 14 (50%) for business. Because you've used at least 50% of your time for business, you can deduct 50% or $600 of your transportation costs. Since you spent $2500 during the conference, this amount qualifies as a deductible destination cost. The $200 you spent during meetings also constitutes deductible destinations costs. Just be sure to write off only 50% of these expenses if they were for meals or entertainment.

Table 6

Expense #	Expense Type	Expense Amount	Deductible (y/n)	Notes
7	Mileage	$ 8.63	Yes	15 mi * 57.5 cents
8	Travel	N/A	No	
9	Travel	N/A	No	
10	Travel (transportation)	$ 600.00	Yes	50% of $1200 (international travel)
	Travel (destination)	$ 2,500.00	Yes	conference (only 50% for meals/entertainment)
	Travel (destination)	$ 200.00	Yes	meetings (only 50% for meals/entertainment)

glossary

Accrual-Based Accounting-
This accounting method is centered on the basis of the flow of goods and services in and out of the business, as opposed to the flow of cash in and out of the business (Cash-Based Accounting).

Actual Expense Method-
An alternative to the standard mileage rate method for calculating the expense of business travel. This method requires comprehensive record keeping on all expenses occurred through the use of a vehicle for business travel.

Automated Under-Reporter Program-
A tool the IRS uses to identify individuals and businesses that under-report their tax liabilities. If the Automated Under-Reporter Program identifies your business, then the IRS files of a form CP2000, which is a notice of proposed changes to your return.

Balance Sheet-
A snapshot of a business's total asset, liability, and equity value at a certain date. A properly rendered balance sheet depicts tax liability in relation to a business's other liabilities.

Cash-Based Accounting-
This accounting method uses the inflow and outflow of cash as the primary basis for a business's accounting records. While accrual-based accounting is generally the best choice for general financial management purposes, cash-based accounting is preferred for establishing tax liability.

C Corporation-
A type of business entity that is recognized as separate from its owners in terms of liabilities. If a C corporation incurs debt or is sued, its shareholders (owners) may not be held personally liable. A C corporation reports its income using a Form 1120 U.S. Corporation Income Tax Return.

Destination Expenses-
Expenses incurred at the site of a business travel destination, such as meals, hotel, rental car, taxi, and other on-site expenses.

Electronic Federal Tax Payment System-
A government system that connects to private bank accounts and allows businesses to submit regular tax payments. Payments can be submitted either online or over the phone.

Employer Identification Number -
A number the IRS issues to a business that's used to keep track of the business's reporting to the IRS and other state agencies.

Estimated Tax-
Refers to the payment of tax from income not subject to withholding, such as tax paid from income gained through self-employment.

Federal Unemployment Tax Act-
A law that levies a 6% tax on employers to help fund workforce agencies that provide benefits to the unemployed (Unemployment Insurance) and assists them in finding new jobs (job service programs).

LLC (Limited Liability Company)-
LLC's owner(s) are not personally liable for debts or legal judgments levied against the company. For tax purposes, LLCs report their profits/losses on either a Form 1040 or 1065 depending on whether it's a single or multi-member LLC. LLCs are considered "pass-through entities"

Lookback Period-
The four quarters ending on June 30th of the previous calendar year. The total amount of deposited payroll taxes during these four quarters determines whether or not your business is required to deposit payroll taxes on a monthly or biweekly basis.

Partnership-
A business entity whereby two or more parties are the exclusive owners of the business. Partners in a business are personally liable for all debts and legal judgments levied against the business. Partnerships must file a Form 1065 "US Return of Partnership Income." For tax purposes, partnerships are considered "pass-through entities" (see the corresponding entry in this glossary).

Pass-Through Entities-
Business entities such as sole proprietorships, partnerships, and LLCs that, unlike corporations, do not pay tax at the entity level. The profits of these entities are passed through to their owners, who then pay standard income taxes.

Sales Tax-
A consumption-based tax added to the price of a good or service. Sales taxes are paid by the consumer when a consumable is purchased.

S Corporation-
An S corporation, unlike a C corporation, is considered a pass-through entity. The corporation itself is not taxed, but only the owners (shareholders) are taxed on their personal income statements based on the profit/loss reported by the S corporation on its Form 1120.

Section 179 Tax Deduction-
A modification of the tax code that allows businesses to deduct the full purchase price of new equipment rather than just deducting the depreciation of the equipment on a year-by-year basis.

Self-Employment Tax-
A federal tax imposed on self-employed individuals to cover their full share of Social Security and Medicare expenses. For 2014, the self-employment tax rate was 15.3% (12.4% for Social Security and 2.9% for Medicare).

Sole Proprietorship-
A business entity owned by a single individual, for which the individual is personally liable for all debts and legal judgments levied against the business. Sole proprietorship owners file a Schedule C with their tax returns to report the profits and losses of the business. For tax purposes, Sole proprietorships are considered "pass-through entities" (see the corresponding entry in this glossary).

Standard Mileage Rate-
The IRS-approved per mile rate used to calculate the business expense of travel by car. In 2016, the standard mileage rate is 54 cents per mile.

Substitute For Return (SFR)-
A tax filing completed by the IRS when an individual or business fails to complete its own tax return.

Tax Credit-
A dollar-for-dollar decrease in the total amount of tax due from a person or business.

Tax Deductions-
A reduction in a person or business's total taxable income.

TFRP-
The IRS assesses a Trust Fund Recovery Penalty against persons responsible for a business's failure to collect or submit its payroll taxes. The TFRP is also known as the 100% penalty, because the penalty is 100% or double the amount of missing payroll taxes.

Transportation Costs-
Costs incurred specifically while getting from one destination to another, such as airfare, bus fare, or a long distance car rental; separate from destination costs.

Use Tax-
An excise tax on a good or service that's used or stored in a certain state, but was purchased outside of the state at a location where sales tax was not collected.

about clydebank

We are a multi-media publishing company that provides reliable, high-quality and easily accessible information to a global customer base. Developed out of the need for beginner-friendly content that is accessible across multiple formats, we deliver reliable, up-to-date, high-quality information through our multiple product offerings.

Through our strategic partnerships with some of the world's largest retailers, we are able to simplify the learning process for customers around the world, providing them with an authoritative source of information for the subjects that matter to them. Our end-user focused philosophy puts the satisfaction of our customers at the forefront of our mission. We are committed to creating multi-media products that allow our customers to learn what they want, when they want and how they want.

ClydeBank Business is a division of the multimedia-publishing firm ClydeBank Media LLC. ClydeBank Media's goal is to provide affordable, accessible information to a global market through different forms of media such as eBooks, paperback books and audio books. Company divisions are based on subject matter, each consisting of a dedicated team of researchers, writers, editors and designers.

For more information, please visit us at :
www.clydebankmedia.com
or contact *info@clydebankmedia.com*

Your world, simplified.

notes

REMEMBER TO DOWNLOAD
YOUR FREE DIGITAL ASSETS!

Visit the URL below to access your free Digital Asset files
that are included with the purchase of this book.

☑ **Summaries**   ☑ **White Papers**
☑ **Cheat Sheets**   ☑ **Charts & Graphs**
☑ **Articles**   ☑ **Reference Materials**

DOWNLOAD YOURS HERE:

www.clydebankmedia.com/taxes-assets

DOWNLOAD A FREE AUDIOBOOK

Get a __FREE__ ClydeBank Media Audiobook + 30 Day Free Trial to Audible.com

Get titles like this absolutely free :

- Business Plan QuickStart Guide
- Options Trading QuickStart Guide
- ITIL For Beginners
- Scrum QuickStart Guide
- JavaScript QuickStart Guide
- 3D Printing QuickStart Guide

- LLC QuickStart Guide
- Lean Six Sigma QuickStart Guide
- Project Management QuickStart Guide
- Social Security QuickStart Guide
- Medicare QuickStart Guide
- And Much More!

To sign up & get your FREE audiobook, visit:

www.clydebankmedia.com/free-audiobook

Explore the World of
BUSINESS

TO EXPLORE ALL TITLES, VISIT:

www.clydebankmedia.com/shop

ClydeBank Media is a Proud Sponsor of

Adopt A Classroom.org

AdoptAClassroom.org empowers teachers by providing the classroom supplies and materials needed to help their students learn and succeed. As an award-winning 501(c)(3), AdoptAClassroom.org makes it easy for individual donors and corporate sponsors to donate funds to K-12 classrooms in public, private and charter schools throughout the U.S.

On average, teachers spend $600 of their own money each year to equip their classrooms – 20% of teachers spend more than $1000 annually. Since 1998 AdoptAClassroom.org has raised more than $30 million and benefited more than 4.25 million students. AdoptAClassroom.org holds a 4-star rating from Charity Navigator.

TO LEARN MORE, VISIT ADOPTACLASSROOM.ORG

Lightning Source UK Ltd.
Milton Keynes UK
UKHW022219161219
355506UK00008B/476/P